RESURRECTION

PRECEPTS FOR LIFE

with Kay Arthur

™

WHAT ARE YOU FACING TODAY?

Why are you weeping, are you hurting badly? Are you overwhelmed with a situation that looks hopeless? Have you lost a loved one, been diagnosed with a serious disease, lost a job or threatened by job loss? Is something from your past tormenting you? Have you recently divorced or been separated from an alienated spouse or children? And are you thinking "I'm not going to survive this!"?

Well, beloved, male or female, young or old, I want to let you in on a little secret from the Word—it's called Resurrection Peace and it comes to us from the "Prince of Peace." The way to it, and the only way to it, is through the One who said "I am the way, the truth, and the life; no one comes to the Father but by Me." That "One" was Jesus. He died for you and because He was sinless and perfect, death could not hold Him. It had to let him go. Raised from the dead, He burst forth from the grave in victory over death.

If you put your faith in His death for your sin and His resurrection for your justification, you will be born again and in this life, here and now, God's Word says the peace you will receive from this faith will be "beyond understanding," filled with wonderful things you could never have imagined. This peace transcends and overpowers every anxiety, every fear, every sense of hopelessness from every situation, every crisis, every broken relationship.

Are you ready to receive this peace? Do you want a way out? Do you want light instead of darkness, praise instead of depression, love instead of hate, reconciliation instead of alienation, hope instead of hopelessness?

Then join me in this program as we interact with God's Word inductively. We'll let Him speak to us directly about the peace we can have because of His Resurrection.

Kay

Visit precept.org/resource for more Free Bible Study Resources!

PRECEPTS FOR LIFE™
Study Guide

This Bible study material was designed for use with the TV and Radio teaching program, Precepts for Life™ with renowned Bible study teacher Kay Arthur, a production of Precept Ministries International. This inductive 30-minute daily Bible study program airs on many satellite, cable, and broadcast stations, and on the internet at **www.preceptsforlife.com.**

As with all Inductive Bible studies, the best way to use the material is to complete the assignments in each lesson before listening or watching the PFL program for that day. These programs are also available on DVD and CD at **www.preceptsforlife.com** or by phone (1.800.763.1990 for television viewers or 1.800.734.7707 for radio listeners). For more information about the Precept Inductive Bible Study Method and Precept Ministries International, visit **www.preceptsforlife.com.**

These materials are also useful for Bible study apart from the Precepts for Life™ programs. We hope you'll find them valuable for studying God's Word and that your walk will be strengthened by the life-changing Truth you'll encounter each day.

Resurrection STUDY GUIDE
Published by Precept Ministries of Reach Out, Inc.
P. O. Box 182218
Chattanooga, TN 37422

ISBN–13: 978-1-62119-401-9

RESURRECTION STUDY GUIDE

PROGRAM 1

Resurrection Peace for Every Situation of Life

TODAY'S TEXT
John 19:30—20:17

CROSS-REFERENCES
Mark 15:34

Psalm 34:20

Zechariah 12:10

1. Read John 19:30-42. Underline the phrase *It is finished* in red.

   a. vv. 34-35: What's the significance of blood and water coming out of Jesus? Was anyone an eyewitness to this?

   b. vv. 36-37: What Old Testament prophecies were clearly fulfilled in these events? (See **Cross-references** Psalm 34:20 and Zechariah 12:10.)

2. Now carefully observe John 20:1-17.

   a. vv. 8-9: What did the two disciples not "understand" before they came to the tomb and found it empty?

   b. v. 10: Where did the disciples go after this?

   c. v. 11: Who remained behind?

   d. v. 12: What did this person see and where?

   e. v. 13: Who spoke first? Why was the woman upset?

   f. v. 14: Who did this woman "see" next but did not "know"?

   g. v. 16: What did she call the stranger after He spoke?

PROGRAM 2

Resurrection Peace That Gives Us Hope

TODAY'S TEXT
John 20:13-29

CROSS-REFERENCES
Isaiah 52:14b

Matthew 27:46

Ephesians 1:20-21

1. Read John 20:13-29 marking *Mary* (Magdalene) and pronouns with a light green shade and the *disciples* including synonyms and pronouns with a light yellow shade.

   a. v. 13: What did the two angels ask the "woman"? How did she respond—what was grieving her? Have you grieved over lost loves ones? Why do we do this? What can help? (See 1 Thessalonians 4:13-18.)

   b. v. 15: What did Jesus ask her? What does she say? Do her answers to this question she has asked twice (13, 15) imply that she's expecting a resurrection? What does she want to do with her "lord" when she finds him?

   c. v. 16: How does Jesus address her now, compared to how He addressed earlier? How does she address Him?

   d. v. 18: What did Mary tell the disciples when she found them?

   e. v. 19: When did Jesus appear to them? Why had they shut the doors to where they were meeting? Does the text imply a miracle here? If so, how? How did Jesus greet the disciples and why?

   f. v. 24: Who did *not* see Jesus show "His hands and His side" (v. 20)?

   g. v. 25: How did he respond when the other disciples said they had seen the Lord? Was "seeing" going to be enough for him? What did he want to do?

   h. v. 27: What does Jesus tell Thomas to do?

   i. Are believers who have not physically seen Jesus (like us) at any disadvantage? What does Jesus pronounce over them?

PROGRAM 3	Resurrection Peace That Takes the Sting out of Death

TODAY'S TEXT
John 11:1-26, 32
Romans 8:28-29
Hebrews 2:14-15
1 Corinthians 15:53-57

CROSS-REFERENCES
John 5:24
Matthew 1:23
Hebrews 4:15
2 Corinthians 5:21
Ephesians 4:9
Romans 6:9
Luke 10:40-42
Hosea 4:6
Jeremiah 13:11a
Psalm 139:16b
Deuteronomy 32:39b
2 Timothy 1:10
Romans 8:2

1. Read John 11:1-26 marking *death* and all synonyms and pronouns with a black tombstone shaded brown and *resurrection* and *life* and all pronouns with a purple arrow pointing up.
   a. vv. 1-3: How are Mary and Martha related to Lazarus? What else do we know about them? (Cf. Luke 10:40-42.) What was wrong with their brother, what did they do about it, and what was their appeal?
   b. v. 21: How did Martha (v. 21) and Mary (v. 32) respond when Jesus came? What did they think? Was it true? Is God sovereign over death? (See cf. Deuteronomy 32:39b.)
   c. vv. 23-24: How did Martha initially understand Jesus' remark that her brother would rise again? What could she have based this hope on? (See Daniel 12:2; John 5:28-29, 6:44, and 11:4.)
   d. v. 25: How does Jesus respond to this long-term hope of hers? Can He raise someone from the dead any time He wants?
   e. v. 26: In what sense is "Everyone who lives and believes in Me will never die" true?

2. Read Hebrews 2:14-15. Mark *devil* with a red pitchfork and *death* with a black tombstone shaded brown.
   a. v. 14: Who had the power of death but lost it? How did he lose it? How did Jesus render him powerless?

3. Now read 1 Corinthians 15:53-57 marking *perishable, death* and *mortality* with a black tombstone shaded brown and *imperishable, life, immortality,* and *victory* with a purple arrow pointing upward.
   a. What's being contrasted in these verses?
   b. What happens to death in the resurrection?

PROGRAM 4	Resurrection Peace That Prepares You to Meet God

TODAY'S TEXT
Acts 2:22-24
Romans 4:23—5:1
Philippians 1:19-24

CROSS-REFERENCES
Acts 2:27
Romans 6:23
2 Corinthians 5:8b

1. Read Acts 2:22-24 marking *nailed to a cross* and *death* including pronouns with a black tombstone shaded brown and *raised* with a purple arrow pointed upward.
   a. Who performed miracles, wonders, and signs through this "man" named Jesus?
   b. What attributes of God delivered Jesus over?

2. Why was it impossible for death to hold Jesus? According to Acts 2:27 and Romans 6:23, why didn't death have a claim on Him? What attribute is death powerless against?

3. Now read Romans 4:23—5:1 marking *credited* with a green plus sign, *believe* and *faith* with an open purple book shaded yellow, *raised* with a purple arrow pointed upward, and *peace* with a purple dove (bird).
   a. For whose sake was Abraham's faith credited as righteousness?
   b. How does "faith credited as righteousness" benefit us too? What do we "share" with Abraham? What do we put our faith in?

4. Now read Philippians 1:19-24 marking *death* and *die* with a black tombstone shaded brown and shading green *life* and *live.*
   a. How does Paul want to honor Christ in his body? How would he actually do this in each case? What does he contrast "shame" with?
   b. How does Paul define "life"? What does this mean? Is death a "loss" for him?
   c. What options face him? Why is the choice between them difficult? Which option is preferable for him *personally?* How is "depart" defined by the context (earlier verses)? What is death for the believer?

PROGRAM 5 — Resurrection Peace That Delivers You From The Pain of Past Sins

TODAY'S TEXT
2 Corinthians 5:01-10;
14-17; 18-21
Romans 6:5-11; 8:12-13

CROSS-REFERENCES
1 Corinthians 15:3-4
Ephesians 1:14
Romans 6:4; 5:8
Hebrews 11:6
Romans 5:20; 4:25

1. Read 2 Corinthians 5:1-10 putting a box around all references to our *earthly house* and an oval around all references to our *heavenly house*.
   a. List what you learn about our *earthly house* and our *heavenly house* in two columns:
   b. How do these truths encourage Paul? What is Paul's preference?

2. Now read 2 Corinthians 5:14-17 marking references to *death* and all synonyms with a black tombstone shaded brown and shading references to *life* and all synonyms green.
   a. What happened when Christ died? What is the result?

3. Next read 2 Corinthians 5:18-21 and shade *reconciliation / reconciled* yellow and *sin* and all synonyms brown.
   a. According to these verses what did God do when Christ died?
   b. What does Paul say he is, and what appeal does he make toward the Corinthians?

4. Last, read Romans 6:5-11 and 8:12-13 marking *death* and all synonyms with a black tombstone shaded brown; shade *sin* brown and *life* and all synonyms green, and mark *resurrection / raised from the dead* with a purple arrow pointed upward.
   a. What do you learn about our old self and sin?
   b. How should we now live? Why?

John 19:30-42

30 Therefore when Jesus had received the sour wine, He said, "It is finished!" And He bowed His head and gave up His spirit.

31 Then the Jews, because it was the day of preparation, so that the bodies would not remain on the cross on the Sabbath (for that Sabbath was a high day), asked Pilate that their legs might be broken, and that they might be taken away.

32 So the soldiers came, and broke the legs of the first man and of the other who was crucified with Him;

33 but coming to Jesus, when they saw that He was already dead, they did not break His legs.

34 But one of the soldiers pierced His side with a spear, and immediately blood and water came out.

35 And he who has seen has testified, and his testimony is true; and he knows that he is telling the truth, so that you also may believe.

36 For these things came to pass to fulfill the Scripture, "NOT A BONE OF HIM SHALL BE BROKEN."

37 And again another Scripture says, "THEY SHALL LOOK ON HIM WHOM THEY PIERCED."

38 After these things Joseph of Arimathea, being a disciple of Jesus, but a secret *one* for fear of the Jews, asked Pilate that he might take away the body of Jesus; and Pilate granted permission. So he came and took away His body.

39 Nicodemus, who had first come to Him by night, also came, bringing a mixture of myrrh and aloes, about a hundred pounds *weight.*

40 So they took the body of Jesus and bound it in linen wrappings with the spices, as is the burial custom of the Jews.

41 Now in the place where He was crucified there was a garden, and in the garden a new tomb in which no one had yet been laid.

42 Therefore because of the Jewish day of preparation, since the tomb was nearby, they laid Jesus there.

John 20:1-17

1 Now on the first day of the week Mary Magdalene came early to the tomb, while it was still dark, and saw the stone already taken away from the tomb.

2 So she ran and came to Simon Peter and to the other disciple whom Jesus loved, and said to them, "They have taken away the Lord out of the tomb, and we do not know where they have laid Him."

3 So Peter and the other disciple went forth, and they were going to the tomb.

4 The two were running together; and the other disciple ran ahead faster than Peter and came to the tomb first;

5 and stooping and looking in, he saw the linen wrappings lying *there;* but he did not go in.

6 And so Simon Peter also came, following him, and entered the tomb; and he saw the linen wrappings lying *there,*

7 and the face-cloth which had been on His head, not lying with the linen wrappings, but rolled up in a place by itself.

8 So the other disciple who had first come to the tomb then also entered, and he saw and believed.

9 For as yet they did not understand the Scripture, that He must rise again from the dead.

10 So the disciples went away again to their own homes.

11 But Mary was standing outside the tomb weeping; and so, as she wept, she stooped and looked into the tomb;

12 and she saw two angels in white sitting, one at the head and one at the feet, where the body of Jesus had been lying.

13 And they said to her, "Woman, why are you weeping?" She said to them, "Because they have taken away my Lord, and I do not know where they have laid Him."

14 When she had said this, she turned around and saw Jesus standing *there,* and did not know that it was Jesus.

15 Jesus said to her, "Woman, why are you weeping? Whom are you seeking?" Supposing Him to be the gardener, she said to Him, "Sir, if you have carried Him away, tell me where you have laid Him, and I will take Him away."

16 Jesus said to her, "Mary!" She turned and said to Him in Hebrew, "Rabboni!" (which means, Teacher).

17 Jesus said to her, "Stop clinging to Me, for I have not yet ascended to the Father; but go to My brethren and say to them, 'I ascend to My Father and your Father, and My God and your God.' "

John 20:13-29

13 And they said to her, "Woman, why are you weeping?" She said to them, "Because they have taken away my Lord, and I do not know where they have laid Him."

14 When she had said this, she turned around and saw Jesus standing *there,* and did not know that it was Jesus.

15 Jesus said to her, "Woman, why are you weeping? Whom are you seeking?" Supposing Him to be the gardener, she said to Him, "Sir, if you have carried Him away, tell me where you have laid Him, and I will take Him away."

16 Jesus said to her, "Mary!" She turned and said to Him in Hebrew, "Rabboni!" (which means, Teacher).

17 Jesus said to her, "Stop clinging to Me, for I have not yet ascended to the Father; but go to My brethren and say to them, 'I ascend to My Father and your Father, and My God and your God."

18 Mary Magdalene came, announcing to the disciples, "I have seen the Lord," and that He had said these things to her.

19 So when it was evening on that day, the first *day* of the week, and when the doors were shut where the disciples were, for fear of the Jews, Jesus came and stood in their midst and said to them, "Peace be with you."

20 And when He had said this, He showed them both His hands and His side. The disciples then rejoiced when they saw the Lord.

21 So Jesus said to them again, "Peace *be* with you; as the Father has sent Me, I also send you."

22 And when He had said this, He breathed on them and said to them, "Receive the Holy Spirit.

23 "If you forgive the sins of any, *their sins* have been forgiven them; if you retain the *sins* of any, they have been retained."

24 But Thomas, one of the twelve, called Didymus, was not with them when Jesus came.

25 So the other disciples were saying to him, "We have seen the Lord!" But he said to them, "Unless I see in His hands the imprint of the nails, and put my finger into the place of the nails, and put my hand into His side, I will not believe."

26 After eight days His disciples were again inside, and Thomas with them. Jesus came, the doors having been shut, and stood in their midst and said, "Peace *be* with you."

27 Then He said to Thomas, "Reach here with your finger, and see My hands; and reach here your hand and put it into My side; and do not be unbelieving, but believing."

28 Thomas answered and said to Him, "My Lord and my God!"

29 Jesus said to him, "Because you have seen Me, have you believed? Blessed are they who did not see, and yet believed."

John 11:1-26, 32

1 Now a certain man was sick, Lazarus of Bethany, the village of Mary and her sister Martha.

2 It was the Mary who anointed the Lord with ointment, and wiped His feet with her hair, whose brother Lazarus was sick.

3 So the sisters sent *word* to Him, saying, "Lord, behold, he whom You love is sick."

4 But when Jesus heard *this,* He said, "This sickness is not to end in death, but for the glory of God, so that the Son of God may be glorified by it."

5 Now Jesus loved Martha and her sister and Lazarus.

6 So when He heard that he was sick, He then stayed two days *longer* in the place where He was.

7 Then after this He said to the disciples, "Let us go to Judea again."

8 The disciples said to Him, "Rabbi, the Jews were just now seeking to stone You, and are You going there again?"

9 Jesus answered, "Are there not twelve hours in the day? If anyone walks in the day, he does not stumble, because he sees the light of this world.

10 "But if anyone walks in the night, he stumbles, because the light is not in him."

11 This He said, and after that He said to them, "Our friend Lazarus has fallen asleep; but I go, so that I may awaken him out of sleep."

12 The disciples then said to Him, "Lord, if he has fallen asleep, he will recover."

13 Now Jesus had spoken of his death, but they thought that He was speaking of literal sleep.

14 So Jesus then said to them plainly, "Lazarus is dead,

15 and I am glad for your sakes that I was not there, so that you may believe; but let us go to him."

16 Therefore Thomas, who is called Didymus, said to *his* fellow disciples, "Let us also go, so that we may die with Him."

17 So when Jesus came, He found that he had already been in the tomb four days.

18 Now Bethany was near Jerusalem, about two miles off;

19 and many of the Jews had come to Martha and Mary, to console them concerning *their* brother.

20 Martha therefore, when she heard that Jesus was coming, went to meet Him, but Mary stayed at the house.

21 Martha then said to Jesus, "Lord, if You had been here, my brother would not have died.

22 "Even now I know that whatever You ask of God, God will give You."

23 Jesus said to her, "Your brother will rise again."

24 Martha said to Him, "I know that he will rise again in the resurrection on the last day."

25 Jesus said to her, "I am the resurrection and the life; he who believes in Me will live even if he dies,

26 and everyone who lives and believes in Me will never die. Do you believe this?"

32 Therefore, when Mary came where Jesus was, she saw Him and fell at His feet, saying to Him, "Lord, if you had been here, my brother would not have died."

Hebrews 2:14-15

14 Therefore, since the children share in flesh and blood, He Himself likewise also partook of the same, that through death He might render powerless him who had the power of death, that is, the devil,

15 and might free those who through fear of death were subject to slavery all their lives.

1 Corinthians 15:53-57

53 For this perishable must put on the imperishable, and this mortal must put on immortality.

54 But when this perishable will have put on the imperishable, and this mortal will have put on immortality, then will come about the saying that is written, "DEATH IS SWALLOWED UP in victory.

55 "O DEATH, WHERE IS YOUR VICTORY? O DEATH, WHERE IS YOUR STING?"

56 The sting of death is sin, and the power of sin is the law;

57 but thanks be to God, who gives us the victory through our Lord Jesus Christ.

Acts 2:22-24

22 "Men of Israel, listen to these words: Jesus the Nazarene, a man attested to you by God with miracles and wonders and signs which God performed through Him in your midst, just as you yourselves know—

23 this Man, delivered over by the predetermined plan and foreknowledge of God, you nailed to a cross by the hands of godless men and put Him to death.

24 "But God raised Him up again, putting an end to the agony of death, since it was impossible for Him to be held in its power.

Romans 4:23—5:1

23 Now not for his [Abraham's] sake only was it written that it was credited to him,

24 but for our sake also, to whom it will be credited, as those who believe in Him who raised Jesus our Lord from the dead,

25 He who was delivered over because of our transgressions, and was raised because of our justification.

5:1 Therefore, having been justified by faith, we have peace with God through our Lord Jesus Christ,

Philippians 1:19-24

19 for I know that this will turn out for my deliverance through your prayers and the provision of the Spirit of Jesus Christ,

20 according to my earnest expectation and hope, that I will not be put to shame in anything, but that with all boldness, Christ will even now, as always, be exalted in my body, whether by life or by death.

21 For to me, to live is Christ and to die is gain.

22 But if I am to live on in the flesh, this will mean fruitful labor for me; and I do not know which to choose.

23 But I am hard-pressed from both directions, having the desire to depart and be with Christ, for that is very much better;

24 yet to remain on in the flesh is more necessary for your sake

2 Corinthians 5:1-10

1 For we know that if the earthly tent which is our house is torn down, we have a building from God, a house not made with hands, eternal in the heavens.

2 For indeed in this *house* we groan, longing to be clothed with our dwelling from heaven,

3 inasmuch as we, having put it on, will not be found naked.

4 For indeed while we are in this tent, we groan, being burdened, because we do not want to be unclothed but to be clothed, so that what is mortal will be swallowed up by life.

5 Now He who prepared us for this very purpose is God, who gave to us the Spirit as a pledge.

6 Therefore, being always of good courage, and knowing that while we are at home in the body we are absent from the Lord—

7 For we walk by faith, not by sight—

8 we are of good courage, I say, and prefer rather to be absent from the body and to be at home with the Lord.

9 Therefore we also have as our ambition, whether at home or absent, to be pleasing to Him.

10 for we must all appear before the judgment seat of Christ, so that each one may be recompensed for his deeds in the body, according to what he has done, whether good or bad.

2 Corinthians 5:14-21

14 For the love of Christ controls us, having concluded this, that one died for all, therefore all died;

15 and He died for all, so that they who live might no longer live for themselves, but for Him who died and rose again on their behalf.

16 Therefore from now on we recognize no one according to the flesh; even though we have known Christ according to the flesh, yet now we know Him in this way no longer.

17 Therefore if anyone is in Christ, he is a new creature; the old things passed away; behold, new things have come.

18 Now all *these* things are from God, who reconciled us to Himself through Christ and gave us the ministry of reconciliation,

19 namely, that God was in Christ reconciling the world to Himself, not counting their trespasses against them, and He has committed to us the word of reconciliation.

20 Therefore, we are ambassadors for Christ, as though God were making an appeal through us; we beg you on behalf of Christ, be reconciled to God.

21 He made Him who knew no sin to be sin on our behalf, so that we might become the righteousness of God in Him.

Romans 6:5-11

5 For if we have become united with Him in the likeness of His death, certainly we shall also be in the likeness of His resurrection,

6 knowing this, that our old self was crucified with Him, in order that our body of sin might be done away with, so that we would no longer be slaves to sin;

7 for he who has died is freed from sin.

8 Now if we have died with Christ, we believe that we shall also live with Him,

9 knowing that Christ, having been raised from the dead, is never to die again; death no longer is master over Him.

10 For the death that He died, He died to sin once for all; but the life that He lives, He lives to God.

11 Even so consider yourselves to be dead to sin, but alive to God in Christ Jesus.

Romans 8:12-13

12 So then, brethren, we are under obligation, not to the flesh, to live according to the flesh—

13 for if you are living according to the flesh, you must die; but if by the Spirit you are putting to death the deeds of the body, you will live.

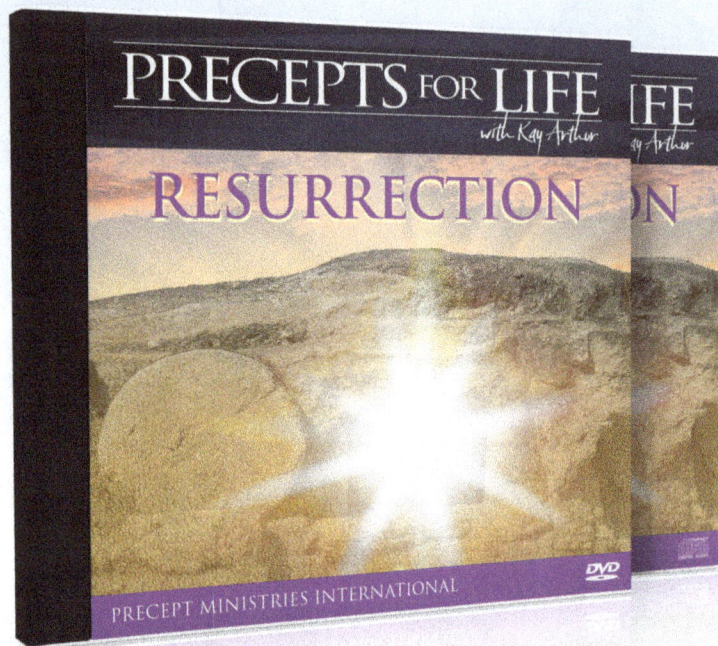

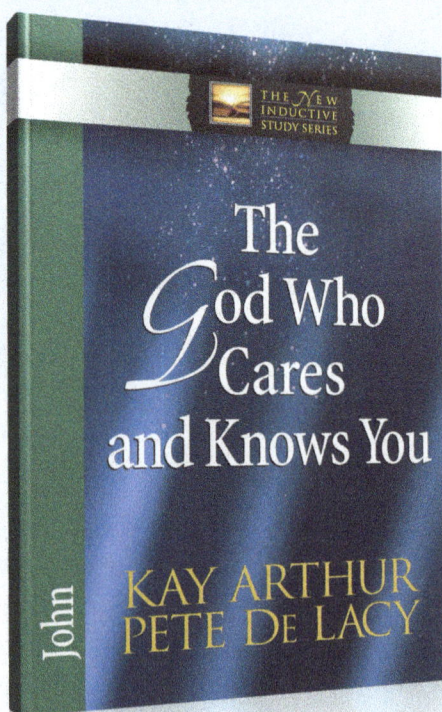

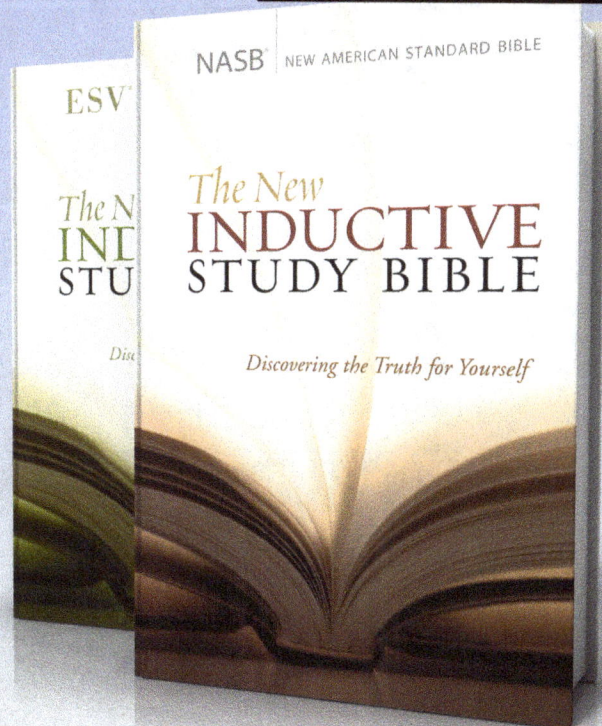

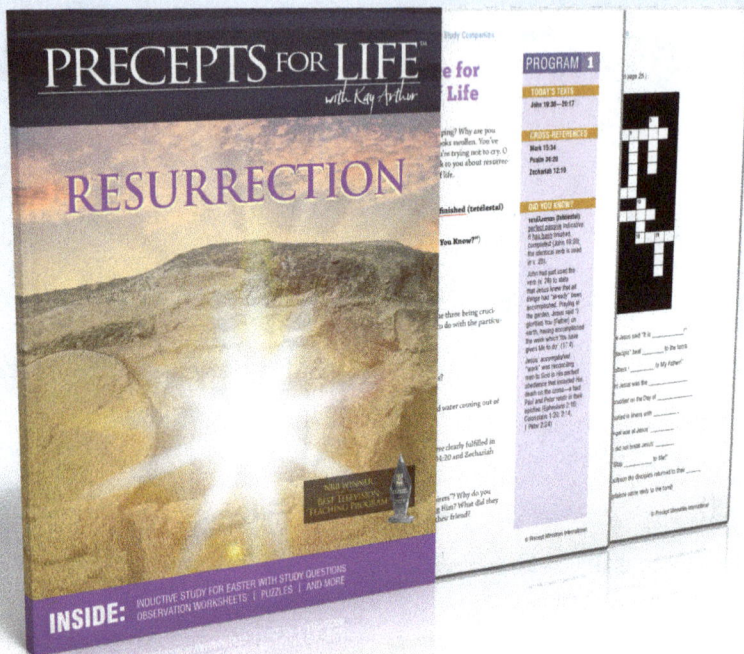

DISCOVER TRUTH FOR YOURSELF

Our passion is for you to discover Truth for yourself through Inductive Bible Study—a unique Bible study method you'll discover in the following pages and use throughout this study, as we engage this important topic together verse by verse.

You can't do a better thing than sit at Jesus' feet, listening to His every word. God's Word, the Bible, has answers for every situation you'll face in life. Listen to what God is saying to you, face-to-face, with truth to transform your life!

INDUCTIVE BIBLE STUDY METHOD

To study and understand God's Word, we use the Inductive Bible Study Method at Precept Ministries International. The Bible is our main source of truth. Before looking for insights from people and commentaries *about* the Bible, we get into the Word of God, beginning with observing the text.

❶ Observation

This is a very interactive process, well worth the time because the truths you discover for yourself will be accurate and profound. It begins by asking the five W and H questions.

Who is speaking? Who is this about? Who are the main characters? And to whom is the speaker speaking?

What subjects and/or events are covered in the chapter? What do you learn about the people, the events, and the teachings from the text? What instructions are given?

When did or will the events recorded occur?

Where did or will this happen? Where was it said?

Why is something said? Why will an event occur? Why this time, person, and/or place?

How will it happen? How will it be done? How is it illustrated?

Careful observation leads to interpretation—discovering what the text means.

❷ Interpretation

The more you observe, the greater you'll understand God's Word. Since Scripture is the best interpreter of Scripture, you and I will be looking at contexts and cross-references to enhance our understanding of the meaning of God's message.

Where should observation and interpretation lead? Application.

❸ Application

After we've observed the text and discovered what it means, we need to think and live accordingly. The result is a transformed life—the more you and I are in the Word of God and adjusting our thinking and behavior to its precepts for life, the more we are changed into the likeness of Jesus Christ! He is the living Word of God who became flesh, the Savior of the world, our coming King of kings!

SO WHERE DO YOU BEGIN?

The Bible is *God's* book, His Word, so when you study it you need to seek the Author's help. Begin with prayer, asking God to lead you into all truth, then open the Study Companion. (We suggest you work one program ahead of the broadcast to get the most out of the study.) Look at the general layout of each day's program and you will find the following:

- Introduction—usually with a challenging question
- Questions that contain pointers on using the Inductive Bible Study Method
- **Where's That Verse?** section containing the Primary Study Passage and several cross-references related to the topic
- Concluding Prayer

WHAT'S NEXT?

- In some programs, I'll point out key words to mark. You'll find many of them on the back cover of this Study Companion with *suggested* colors and symbols to spot them quickly in the text. Color coding key words helps you identify and recall. We have included a cutout bookmark so you can remember to mark each key word the same way throughout the text.

  You can mark these key words before or after the program, whichever is easier. You can also get the CD or DVD of the program and mark the key words later while studying.

Feel free to mark them your own way—there's nothing sacred about the particular symbols and colors I use!

- The cross-references I mention in these programs are under **Where's That Verse?** After you read them, you can jot them in the margins of the **Observation Worksheets** or write them in the wide margins of your Bible. I suggest you first pencil them in, then write them in ink later.

- For book studies, you'll find an **At A Glance** chart in the back. After we complete a chapter, record a summary theme there and in the space provided in your **Observation Worksheets**. Themes help you remember main ideas of chapters **At A Glance** after you finish the study. You'll also find these charts after each book in the *New Inductive Study Bible*.

MISSED A PROGRAM?

- Go to our website at **www.PreceptsForLife.com**. TV viewers can call 1.800.763.1990 and radio listeners 1.888.734.7707 to learn how to find programs online.

GETTING THE MOST FROM THIS STUDY

- Try to stay one program ahead of me so you'll learn directly from the Word of God and our time together will be like a "discussion group," as we reason together through the Scriptures. You'll get much more out of our time together if you've done this preparation.

- Try to memorize a key verse for every program covered. God will bring these to your remembrance when you need them!

- Pray about what you learn each day. Ask God to remind you of these truths and give you another person to share them with. These two exercises will do amazing things in your life.

- Get the CD or DVD set of this series and listen when you get ready for work in the morning, do chores around the house, or have family devotions. Or listen with an open Bible and discuss the teaching and its application to your life. Get together with a friend, view or listen to a message, and discuss it or use it for family devotions. You can also view or listen programs online. Visit **www.PreceptsForLife.com.**

- Request Precept's mailings to stay abreast of what God is doing around the world and to pray for the needs we share with you. You can be a significant part of this unique global ministry God is using to establish people in His Word. Here are some items you can request:

- ✦ The *Plumbline*—Precept Ministry's monthly e-newsletter that keeps you up to date on Bible study topics, products and events that help you in your walk with Christ.

- ✦ A prayer list so you can partner with us in prayer for our ministries in nearly 150 countries and 70 languages.

- ✦ "Inside information" each month when you join our "E-Team" of regular prayer and financial supporters. Visit **www.PreceptsForLife.com** for more information on how you can support our programs. (You can check out the current monthly letter right now on our website.)

- ✦ Advance notice of conferences at our headquarters in Chattanooga and throughout the United States and Canada.

- ✦ Information about our study tours in Israel, Jordan, Greece, Turkey, and Italy, where we teach various books of the Bible right where the action occurred!

- We use one of the most accurate translations of the Bible, the New American Standard (Updated). If the topic is a book study, our **Observation Worksheets** will contain the complete text. Since you'll be instructed to mark words and phrases and make notes in the text, you'll want to have colored pencils or pens available. As you grow in inductive study skills, you may want to use your Bible instead. We believe the best Bible to use is the *New Inductive Study Bible.* See our back pages to find out more about this ultimate study Bible. Now get started!

- Finally, stay in touch with me personally. I'd so love to hear from you by email or letter so I can be sensitive to where you are and what you're experiencing—problems you're wrestling with, questions you have, etc. This will help me teach more effectively and personally. Just email us at info@precept.org. (Don't worry, Beloved, I won't mention you by name; but as you listen, you'll know I've heard you!)

I'm committed to you . . . because of Him. The purpose of the "Precepts For Life" TV & Radio programs is to help you realize your full potential in God, so you can become the exemplary believer God intends you to be...studying the Bible inductively, viewing the world biblically, making disciples intentionally, and serving the Church faithfully in the power of the Holy Spirit."

That's my vision for us as believers! Won't you help us spread it to others?

Looking for people...looking for truth!

How Do I Start Studying The Bible?

Do you wonder,
God, how can I obey You and study your Word? Where do I begin? How can I discover truth for myself?

DISCOVER TRUTH FOR YOURSELF

There are some study tools we would recommend for you to begin with, as each will teach you the inductive method of study. By inductive we mean that you can go straight to the Word of God and discover truth for yourself, so you can say … "for You, Yourself have taught me" (Psalm 119:102).

Let's Get Started! For a jump start on inductive study, we recommend the following:

- *Lord, Teach Me To Study The Bible in 28 Days.* In this hands-on introduction to the basics of inductive study, you'll see why you need to study God's Word and how to dig into the truths of a book of the Bible. The instructions will walk you through the books of Jonah and Jude, and you'll be awed at what you see on your own! Discussion questions are included.

- *God, Are You There? Do You Care? Do You Know About Me?* This 13-week, self-contained inductive study on the Gospel of John is powerful and life-changing. Study the book of John, as you learn and put into practice inductive study skills. The Gospel of John was written that you might believe that Jesus is the Son of God and that believing, might have life in His name. You will know you are loved! Discussion questions are included.

- *How to Study Old Testament History and Prophecy Workshop.* Discover truths about who God is and how He works as you learn to study inductively, step by step, and be challenged to apply these truths to your life. This workshop will give you the tools to study and understand Old Testament history and prophecy. Go to www.precept.org or call 800-763-8280 to find out about workshops in your area, or online training.

- *How to Study a New Testament Letter Workshop.* Grow in the knowledge of the Lord Jesus Christ and His plan for your life. This inductive study workshop will equip you to study the New Testament letters and apply their truths to your life. Go to www.precept. org or call 800-763-8280 to find out about workshops in your area, or online training.

Now that you've begun . . . continue studying inductively using one of these:

- *40 Minute Bible Studies.* These 6-week topical studies are a good for personal study and a great way to start discipling others one-on-one or in a group setting—teaching them who God is, introducing them to Jesus Christ, and helping them learn God's precepts for life. These studies enable you to discover what God says about different issues of life. No homework is necessary for the students prior to group time.

- *The New Inductive Study Series,* now complete covering every book of the Bible, was created to help you discover truth for yourself and go deeper into God's precepts, promises and purposes. This powerful series is ideal for personal study, small groups, Sunday school classes, family devotions, and discipling others. Containing 13-week long studies, the New Inductive Study Series also provides easy planning for church curriculum! You can now survey the entire Bible

- *Lord Series.* These life-changing devotional studies cover in greater depth major issues of our relationship with God and with others, teaching us how to practically live out our faith. Ideal for small groups, these contain discussion guides and teaching DVDs are available for some.

- *Discover 4 Yourself* is a dynamic series of inductive studies for children. Children who can read learn how to discover truth for themselves through the life-impacting skills of observation, interpretation, and application. You'll be amazed at the change that comes when children know for themselves what the Word of God says! Teach them now so they can stand firm in a first-hand knowledge of truth as they hit their teen years. This award-winning series is popular in Christian schools and among homeschoolers. Teacher's guides are available online.

- *The New Inductive Study Bible (NISB)* is a unique and exciting! Most study Bibles give you someone else's interpretation of the text. The NISB doesn't tell you what to believe, rather it helps you discover truth for yourself by showing you how to study inductively and providing instructions, study helps, and application questions for each book of the Bible, as well as wide margins for your notes. It's filled with many wonderful features that will guide you toward the joy of discovering the truths of God's Word for yourself. This Bible is your legacy.

GO DEEPER WITH OTHERS...
IN SMALL GROUP BIBLE STUDIES

Join others in the study of God's Word, sharing insights from the Scripture and discussing application to your life. Each of the studies described above are appropriate for groups as well as for individual study.

Discussion questions are included, so that you can dialogue about what you're learning with a group. These studies will teach you what it means to live by God's Word—and how it is applied to life. Learn about and discuss with others the truth that sets you free! To find out about inductive Bible study groups in your area, go to www.precept.org or call 800-763-8280.

DISCIPLE

How can you help others study God's Word inductively? Use the studies described above to share with others—one-on-one or in a small group. Lead others in discovering truth for themselves and experience the joy of seeing God change lives!

If you want training in how to lead these and other Precept Upon Precept studies go to www.precept.org or call us at 800-763-8280.

Precept Ministries International | P.O. Box 182218 | Chattanooga, TN 37422
800.763.8280 | www.precept.org